The front cover illustration is taken from an 18th century engraving said to be of Gravesend's first parish church, St Mary's, Pelham Road by an unknown artist. The illustration is based on what remained of the building before the stones were used to repair the nearby road in 1797.

As far as I can establish, there is no other known image of the original church.

The History of Medieval Gravesend

The History of Medieval Gravesend

Toni Mount

Echoes from History

Contents

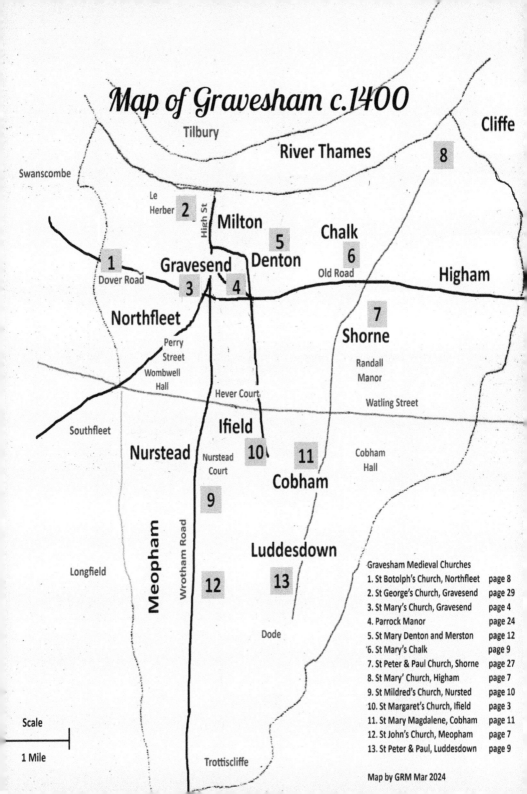

Map of Gravesham c.1400

Tilbury

River Thames

Cliffe

Swanscombe

Le Herber **2**

High St

Milton

8

Gravesend

Chalk

Denton **5**

6

1

Dover Road

3 **4**

Old Road

Higham

Northfleet

7

Perry Street

Shorne

Wombwell Hall

Randall Manor

Hever Court

Watling Street

Southfleet

Ifield

Nurstead

Nurstead Court

10

11

Cobham Hall

Cobham

9

Meopham

Wrotham Road

Luddesdown

Longfield

12

13

Dode

Scale

1 Mile

Trottiscliffe

Gravesham Medieval Churches
1. St Botolph's Church, Northfleet — page 8
2. St George's Church, Gravesend — page 29
3. St Mary's Church, Gravesend — page 4
4. Parrock Manor — page 24
5. St Mary Denton and Merston — page 12
6. St Mary's Chalk — page 9
7. St Peter & Paul Church, Shorne — page 27
8. St Mary' Church, Higham — page 7
9. St Mildred's Church, Nursted — page 10
10. St Margaret's Church, Ifield — page 3
11. St Mary Magdalene, Cobham — page 11
12. St John's Church, Meopham — page 7
13. St Peter & Paul, Luddesdown — page 9

Map by GRM Mar 2024

1

～

The History of Medieval Gravesham

Firstly, let me put to rest an old chestnut: Gravesend did not get its name because it marked the end of the plague graves of London. In fact, the name goes back centuries before the plague came to England to do its worst. However, the name does indicate the extent of the authority of the greeve (or reeve) of London who, from the 10th century was the customs collector for ports upriver on the Thames. So originally, Gravesham was the village belonging to the greeve (Greeve's Ham) and later showed where his authority ended (Greeve's End).

But why is Gravesend here? Many settlements grew up around a river crossing or a market place but Anglo Saxon Gravesend did neither. The rights to a market weren't granted until much later and the first settlement was away from the river, close to where the Pelham Arms Pub now stands. So maybe it developed at the cross-roads? The road east-west from London to Dover crossed by the road from Southfleet and Perry Street heading north to the Thames.

Another medieval structure that has long since disappeared is Hever Court, built by the de Hever family they left the area in the 1300s and built Hever Castle near Edenbridge. The family home of Anne Boleyn the second wife of Henry VIII. Hever Court was in the parish of St Margaret's Ifield which straddles the ancient Roman road Watling Street which passes east/west through the borough.

So much trade took place on the River Thames: it was easier to sail a barge full of stone than to carry it on carts on the non-existent roads. And safer and quicker for people too, avoiding robbers that could hide in a woodland. Looking at a topographical map of the Thames estuary, you will realise that marshes spread along both north and south banks of the river from Lambeth and Southwark, via Thamesmead, Erith and Dartford and then again from Shorne, Higham and Cliffe to the Medway. This is repeated on the north bank via Rainham marshes to Canvey Island. The only high ground east of London to reach down to the river is at Gravesend; a safe, stable place to land or load the busy river traffic. As well as goods, people were transported via the landing stages, strands and wharves that were developed by the river. Medieval Gravesend was a unique riverside port. Perhaps it is surprising, the lack of any Norman defences. The Tudors built defences here and earlier kings had a grand riverfront palace but there were few defences to protect trade from piracy or future French or Spanish invasion.

In this publication we will be looking at the period between the departure of the Romans c.410 AD and the start of the Tudor period 1485 – designated 'medieval'. When discussing the churches and chapels of the area it should be noted that this period is pre-Reformation and therefore everyone would be Roman Catholic, there was no Church of England. This would be created by Henry VIII after his split with the Church of Rome in the 1530s.

2

⌇⌇

St Mary's Church, Gravesend

Sadly, the original parish church of Gravesham, mentioned in Domesday, no longer exists. Dedicated to St Mary, it stood behind where the White Post pub used to be, opposite the main entrance to the Girls Grammar School (now Mayfield Grammar School) in Pelham Road. At the time, Pelham Road was known as Manor Road or Lane, and all the lands on the school side of the road were part of Manor Farm, which was located close to the current junction with Darnley Road. So it seems likely the original Gravesham manor house was in this area, handy for the lord to attend the church opposite. This historic route. Manor Lane, continued down to the river via what is now Bath Street, leading to West Street.

Church land – known as glebe land – was always marked out by white posts: hence the name of the pub and Glebe Road (off Pelham Rd South) must also have belonged to the church. At the present crossroads of Pelham Rd and Dover Road was St Mary's Green with a large pond. Nearby, to the south of the old road, an Anglo-Saxon silver cross, now kept at The British Museum, was found in 1838 in association with a hoard of

522 silver coins, dated 814-898 AD. It seems, in the early part of Graves-end's history, this was the village centre at a crossroads with a lane which led south to the tiny hamlet of Perry Street – where pear trees grew – (now called Old Perry Street, still with its pub and forge) and onward via the Roman settlement of Springhead to Southfleet. Gravesham was a stop-off point by road or river on the journey from London to Canterbury and Dover, avoiding the Watling Street which had no resting places between Dartford and Strood and passed through the notorious woodlands that extended from Cobham to Shorne, where outlaws and cutthroats waylaid unwary travellers.

During the 14th century, Gravesend began to change – including its name – but in the 1377 poll tax returns neither Gravesend, Milton nor Northfleet were yet big enough to be called 'towns'. In other words, there were less than 300 adults paying tax, whereas places like Southfleet, Cobham and Cliffe were classed as towns. The focus of village life in Gravesend was moving away from the Dover Road crossroads towards the River Thames. King Edward III was busy fighting the French in what we call the Hundred Years War and Gravesend was becoming a vital port, both for trade and military purposes, so the inhabitants were moving to live closer to the river. St Mary's church wasn't at the centre of things anymore and when it suffered a serious fire in 1508, it was patched up rather than repaired properly.

Flint walls still exist in the narrow alleyways of Pelham Terrace and Bycliffe Terrace behind where the White Post Pub stood; the remaining mews cottages and boundary walls still cast a shadow of the past. Until the late 18th century, the walls of St Mary's church still stood 4 feet high in places and someone did an etching of what it may have looked like. In 1797, its walls were broken up and used to repair the roads and in 1822, William Crafter measured the site as 325 feet long by 100 feet wide.

Closer to the current town more Saxon remains were discovered when the new community Hospital was built.

3

꩜

The Domesday Manors

You may be surprised to hear that the famous Domesday Book, compiled for William the Conqueror in 1086, lists thirteen manors as part of what is now Gravesham. Gravesend itself was called Gravesham in the survey, which was carried out so the king knew exactly what everyone owned and would get all the taxes due to him. But Gravesham was one of the lesser manors at the time. The area was described in terms of how many oxen would be needed to plough the arable land and how many pigs could be accommodated by the woodland. Today there are very few medieval buildings remaining in the area but the churches of Gravesham give us a small glimpse into the past.

Meopham The largest of the thirteen manors was Meopham which sits atop the North Downs six miles to the south of Gravesham. According to Domesday, it was owned by the monks of Canterbury and needed 30 teams of 8 oxen to plough its 850 acres, as well as having woodland for 10 pigs to forage.

As with many parishes, a church has stood in the same position for over

1000 years. The earliest mention of the village of Meopham was in a deed dated 788 for land in the neighbouring village of Trottiscliffe and in a will, dated around 965 AD, where Byrthic, named as the Lord of the Manor at Meopham, had Wina, the priest from Meopham church, as one of the witnesses.

Most of the current church dates to the 1300s but the earliest parts under the tower and the chancel date to c.1240. The rebuilding was funded by Simon de Meopham, who was born here and later became Archbishop of Canterbury. In 1328 the archbishop issued an 'indulgence', 'whereby 40 days of penances were remitted to all who should visit St John the Baptist's Church in Meopham to confess their sins, walk around the churchyard, say the Paternoster (the Lord's Prayer), and pray for the souls of the archbishop's parents'. This generated income for the Church, as pilgrims on their way to Canterbury could divert to Meopham to earn these indulgences.

In 1382 the aisles of the nave collapsed when the church suffered considerable damage from an earthquake but was rebuilt and by the mid-15th century the church was a significant building, with a large open space that was used for village feasts, markets and dramatic performances.

Higham Situated on the southern bank of the Thames, east of Gravesend and Milton, Higham was the second largest manor. It also included the now-extinct manor of Oakleigh (which is still part of Higham parish), as well as land across the river in Essex. This suggests folk crossed the river to the northern bank as, according to Domesday, they pastured 200 sheep on the Essex side.

The Higham area had grown by 30 acres since Saxon times as locals reclaimed land from the marshes by digging drainage ditches.

Higham Priory, located adjacent to the now unused St Mary's Church in Church Street on the edge of the marshes at the north of the parish, was built on land granted to Mary of Blois, daughter of King Stephen. In 1148, the nuns of St Sulphice-la-Foret, in Brittany, moved to Higham.

The tolls of the old ferry which crossed the river between Lower Higham and East Tilbury in Essex was granted to the nuns and was the only ferry to cross the Thames below Gravesend. From pre-Roman times, ancient approach routes converge on this point where there may have been an earlier ford across the Thames. The priory received tolls from the ferry but was responsible for a causeway and bridge to reach it – the causeway is still visible on the riverside at a point directly opposite Coalhouse Point on the northern bank. St Mary's was in existence on the site before the Norman Conquest. In 1357 the nunnery received a papal indulgence to raise money for repairs. It is thought likely that this was used to build a new south aisle for the church, which is as large as the original nave. The nunnery was closed in 1522

Northfleet This manor on the southern bank of the Thames to the west of Gravesend was known as Fleote by the Saxons c.600 AD, and Flete by 1000 AD. But in Domesday it is recorded as Norfluet, and owned directly by the Archbishop of Canterbury. It was the next largest manor and had a watermill. But it was only a few years later that Northfleet became the largest of the Gravesham manors. Richard, Lord of Tonbridge – an important baron at the time – owned 30 shillings worth of land in Northfleet and 18s 6d worth of land in Meopham too. The watermill would have been in the vicinity of Northfleet Creek where the river Fleet (or Ebbsfleet, which denoted Northfleet and Southfleet) entered the Thames after passing under the bridge at the bottom of Stonebridge Hill.

The parish church of Northfleet (dating from the 14th century, but with work from earlier periods) is located at the highest point of the parish now known as Northfleet Hill and is dedicated to St Botolph. The church contains a 14th-century carved oak screen, which is thought to be the oldest in Kent. The triangular space in front of the church was the village green.

Chalk To the east of Gravesnd on the south bank of the Thames between Milton and Higham, Chalk is combined with the extinct manor of Beckley and also owned land in Essex. This manor came next in size in Domesday. Although Beckley was only worth 15s, King William I himself owned land worth 7s in Chalk: a gift from his brother, Bishop Odo of Bayeux, who owned a lot of land in Kent. Chalk was known as early as the 8th century, when a Witanagemot (a Saxon council meeting) took place here at the church, known as the 'Synod of Chalkhythe' in 785. (Hythe being a name for a landing place so we know that the area had connections with the river).

The current church dates from the 12th century but stands on higher ground a mile or so south of the river and is now separate from the modern village of Chalk but it is likely that the earlier village was closer to the church. Significant work on the church took place in the 13th, 14th and 15th centuries; the font is Norman and the oldest bell was first hung in 1348. The church is a prominent landmark for navigation in the Thames. The parish of Chalk is now entirely agricultural with Filborough the oldest of the farms in the area, having first been mentioned in 1220.

Luddesdown This was the fifth largest manor located south east of Gravesend, nestled in the North Downs. The hamlet was first recorded in 975 as Hludes duna (Hlud's hill); in 939 there was a mound nearby called Hludes beorh – suggesting that Hlud was a prominent local. In Domesday, it was Ludesdon with 300 acres of cultivated land and owning 4 houses in Rochester. Sitting at the head of two, long valleys known as Bowling Alley and Henley Street, the church of St Peter and St Paul remains, alongside a late Norman house and adjacent farm.

Following the church reforms of Henry III, many noblemen rebuilt their own small churches, as in Luddesdown, despite Domesday stating 'there is a church here' the earliest identifiable masonry, in the north and west walls, dates from the 13th century. The south aisle and tower, including an early wooden 'log ladder' and three medieval bells, were built in the 14th century.

The tiny Norman chapel of Dode is found another mile to the south.

Dode village was decimated by the Black Death in 1349 and never recovered. Note that Dode, Luddesdown and Cobham churches lay on a direct north/south alignment, indicating the possible position of a pre-historic 'lay-line'.

Nurstead This manor, situated 3 miles south of Gravesend and just half a mile north of Meopham is listed next in Domesday as Notestede with 240 acres,

Nurstead has a small 14th-century church built of flint and dedicated to Saint Mildred. To the north of the church is Nurstead Court, one of the few remaining medieval houses in the area. It was built in 1320 by Stephen de Gravesend, Bishop of London. The great hall is said to be one of the finest in England, rising 36 feet to the roof. Stephen's new manor belonged to the family so wasn't church property and there was almost certainly an earlier house on the site dating back to the Saxon period. The hall stands within a high wall made of knapped flint with a solar and a tower stands at one corner of the hall. Initially built for defence it was later a chapel.

Milton This manor had 210 acres, according to Domesday. The Church of Sts Peter and Paul dates back to the 14th century but there has been a church in Milton since at least Saxon times. A remnant of the earlier church can be seen low down at the south west corner where a filled-in arch is part of the present structure. The tower at the west end was built later, probably in the early 15th century and the whole is now Grade II listed.

Another listed building is Milton Chantry, founded in 1304 by Aymer de Valence, Earl of Pembroke, great-uncle to the king, Edward II, who granted him the Manor of Milton. The earl specified that the chantry priests must pray for his huge number of relatives for evermore. In 1312, Aymer stood as one of seven godfathers to the future king, Edward III.

Gravesham In 8th place, was the manor of Gravesham with 150 acres. Before the Normans arrived, Gravesham had been the 4th most valuable manor, worth £12, but while other manors improved, by 1086 Gravesham was valued at only £10. Gravesend, situated 20 miles to the east of London, has always been involved in the city's defence. In 1381, despite the erection of a series of warning beacons, a combined French and Spanish force sailed up river as far as Gravesend, burnt the town and carried off many of the inhabitants into slavery.

Cobham Henhurst as it was called at the time of Domesday, came next in the list of manors and lies to the southeast of Gravesend between Chalk and Luddesdown. It was worth just £2 10s.

The parish church of St Mary Magdalene sits on the highest point in the village of Cobham and dominates the village. Early in the 13th century, the de Cobham family began to provide money for rebuilding the existing church. Only the chancel dating from 1220 survives.

The de Cobhams treated Cobham church as their own chapel and used it for many family burials, making it unusually large for a parish church From 1360-70, there was an intense period of building by Sir John de Cobham, who is described on his memorial brass in the church as 'the Founder of this place'. He re-built the nave with its two side aisles, raised the roof and added the porch He also built the attached Cobham College, which still stands to the south of the church. Finally, he added the tower which further lengthened the two aisles. It is possible that the church was designed by Henry Yevele, who was the King Edward III's Master Mason and the architect of the naves of Canterbury Cathedral and Westminster Abbey.

Cobham College was a chantry employing five priests for the purpose of praying for the speedy passage of the soul of John de Cobham (and others) through Purgatory and into Heaven.

Henry de Cobham, was created first Baron Cobham in 1313 as Lord of the Manors of Cobham and of Cooling. There has been a manor house on the site of Cobham Hall since the 12th century but it was rebuilt in Tudor times. (In the 18th century, the hall passed to the Bligh family, later Earls of Darnley.) Cooling Castle was built in the 1380s on the Hoo Peninsula about 6 miles east of Gravesend by the Cobham family to guard the area against French raids into the Thames Estuary. Sir John de Cobham and Sir Robert Knolles (or Knollys), also paid for the building of the new Rochester Bridge in stone across the River Medway, replacing the earlier wooden bridge which was often in need of repair.

Denton and Merston These little manors brought up the rear in Domesday with 60 acres each, although Denton must have had other assets as it was valued at £5 and owned by the Bishop of Rochester, whilst Merston was worth only £2 10s.

It seems Milton, Nurstead, Chalk and Luddesdown and, maybe, Gravesham, had suffered some form of oppression which reduced their value. But Meopham, Northfleet and Denton, being church lands, were spared. In Domesday, there is also a mention of Gravesend-in-Tilbury, owned by a Count Eustace. Whether this was part of Gravesham proper isn't said but there were only two villagers listed there and a plough. It was worth 20s.

At the time of Domesday, all the manors had their own churches with the exceptions of Henhurst (Cobham), Beckley in Chalk and Oakleigh in Higham. There is no record of Cobham church until 1115, although it is said to be built on Saxon foundations, so we don't know why it doesn't get a mention in Domesday. Merston – Green Farm Lane in Lower Shorne – had a church at some time in its history but it isn't recorded in Domesday – perhaps both were exempt, or without a permanent priest. The Norman foundations of Merston Church were found in 1957 at Green Farm, Lower Shorne.

Ferries. In 1380 French and Spanish warships burned Gravesend and many captives were taken. Afterwards, the town was in great distress. The following year King Richard II arrived by water but not liking the 'shabby appearance of the inhabitants, was afraid to land and was rowed back to the Tower'.

Gravesend watermen were granted the exclusive right to ferry passengers to London, in compensation for the burning of the town. This became known as the Long Ferry. Gravesend watermen guarded their right to run a regular service up and down the river with the tide, manned by four oarsmen and a steersman.

The Cross Ferry which still links Gravesend and Tilbury, was originally owned by the Lords of the Manor of Parrock (Milton) and Tilbury. Also, frequent crossings were made at Higham and Chalk where farmers kept sheep on Essex marshes, and Pilgrims crossed en-route to Canterbury.

Woodland. Domesday Book records woodlands which, in medieval times, supplied building timber, fire wood and food for pigs, like acorns and beech nuts. This last use was so important that woodland was measured, not in acres, but by how many pigs it could support. Northfleet and Luddesdown had woods for 20 pigs, Denton enough for 15 and Meopham 10. Milton had 5s worth of woodland, perhaps unsuitable for pigs for some reason. Although no woodland is recorded in Graveham, there must have been some as a later writer mentions the place being famed for its nightingales, which are definitely woodland birds.

Watermills. Windmills were a later invention but watermills were major sources of income for lords of the manor in the 11th century and beyond and, therefore, taxable. The lords often forced villages to use the manor mill and pay to have their corn ground into flour. Some severe lords, like a later Abbot of St Albans for one, would confiscate the villagers' own quern stones so they couldn't grind their corn at home. This particular abbot paved his courtyard with the quern stones but the folk of St Albans broke into his palace and dug them up again during the Peasants' Revolt in 1381. Northfleet and Higham had the largest, most profitable mills taxed at £1 each per year, while Chalk, Beckley-in-Chalk and Milton had smaller ones.

Meadows. Meadows and grazing land were taxed as well. Higham had most with 30 acres, Northfleet 20 and Meopham and Chalk 16. The other manors had less than 12 acres each but Gravesham and Milton had special animal enclosures constructed which get a mention in Domesday. Northfleet and Higham specialised in fishing the Thames but only Gravesham and Milton each had a hythe – a landing stage – which might imply a ferry service of some kind or goods and trading by river.

4

The People of Gravesham

That sums up the manor lands of Gravesham, but what about the people who lived on those lands? In those days there was said to be three 'estates': 'Those who prayed; those who fought and those who laboured' Top of the social heap were those who owned the lands. Ten manors were owned by Odo, Bishop of Bayeux, half-brother to William the Conqueror. Odo owned Gravesham, Milton, Higham and Oakleigh, Chalk and Beckley, Nurstead, Henhurst, Merston and Luddesdown. His power was unrivalled in the area although he rarely visited his manors here. As we've heard, the Archbishop of Canterbury owned Northfleet; the monks of Canterbury owned Meopham and the Bishop of Rochester owned Denton; while the king owned a little bit of land in Chalk and Richard of Tonbridge owned bits of Northfleet and Meopham.

Under these lords came the tenants, though Northfleet and Meopham had no tenants listed. The most important tenant in the whole area was Adam who rented over 1000 acres of land in Chalk, Beckley and Higham. He also had land at Cooling. Ralph, son of Thorold (probably of Danish decent) had 560 acres in Oakleigh, Milton and Luddesdown. Next came Wadard who held 240 acres of land in Nurstead and then Herbert Fitz Ivo who held 150 acres in Gravesham. Ranulf Peverel rented 120 acres of land belonging to Chalk manor which were across the river in Essex. Finally, Helto held 60 acres in Merston (Lower Shorne) and Ansgot of Rochester rented 60 acres in Henhurst (Cobham).

Under these well-off tenants came the villeins or villagers – sort of farmers. They weren't necessarily criminals but the word 'villain' does derive from 'villein'; perhaps the lords liked to think nobody above that rank ever broke the law. In return for his landholding, the villein had to carry out services for his lord and pay rent. Northfleet had 36 villeins; Gravesham only 4. Their rents may have been paid in money but more likely in kind: 2 chickens for his lordship every quarter – that kind of thing. The services for the lord might have been one day a week weeding his crops; three days a week reaping at harvest time; cutting and carrying wood for the lord's fire or taking his surplus crops to market. Whatever the rents and services, everything would have been recorded in the manor rolls.

Bordars or cottagers came next down the social ladder, having just a small plot of land with their cottage, big enough to grow food for the family. With nothing much to spare, all they could give the lord was their labour. Meopham had 71 families of bordars but Gravesham and Northfleet had none. At the bottom of the pile, with no rights whatsoever, were the serfs or slaves. They were counted as the lord's personal property, worth less than his horse and oxen and listed among his furniture. These serfs were sometimes kidnapped foreigners or criminals serving a sentence – a sort of community service – or even the children of borders, if their parents couldn't feed them or couldn't pay the rent any other way. Higham had 20 serfs/slaves, Gravesham 8 and Northfleet 7.

5

～

The King's Manor

In 1362, King Edward III recovered the Manor of Gravesend from Robert de Ufford, Earl of Suffolk, who had died without an heir. The king decided he was going to build a luxurious new house – to be known as Le Herber or The Garden (the language of the king's court was still French) – down by the Thames, rather than further inland where the old Gravesend manor had been. Work began in November 1362 and was completed by August 1368, having cost the king £1,350 to build. The house was of Reigate stone and Kentish ragstone from Maidstone, together with flint, chalk, vast amounts of timber and 61,400 tiles for the roof. Lime for the mortar was made at Northfleet. All building materials came by river, so a new wharf had to be built for unloading these heavy cargoes. At least it wasn't far to the royal construction site: remains of the manor walls were found when slums in West Street were demolished around 1900.

Le Herber had a great hall and a king's chamber: all very grand but the windows probably weren't glazed, just shuttered, as the only glass mentioned is that required for the windows of the chapel. However, there were three purpose-built latrine houses. Thomas Shonk was paid £10 for painting and varnishing the manor, 18 iron candelabra were supplied by Master Stephen atte Tower, along with window bars, hinges and locks. Fireplaces with chimneys were a new invention, replacing hearths in the middle of the floor, and the mason, Maurice Young, was paid to build 7 stone fireplaces, 3 of which definitely had chimneys since John Gardinere was paid for 3 decorative iron firebacks. About a third of the money spent went on timber and carpentry. The king's Master Carpenter, Hugh Herland – who also carved the wonderful hammerbeams in Westminster Hall – worked at Le Herber, as did John of Brampton, the king's Master Glazier, so the finished work must have been impressive. There was a great gatehouse with a roofed chamber above it and living quarters either side, as well as a smaller gate which led out into the king's private park. This park covered 50 acres at least. We know because Roger Giddyng, the priest at St Mary's, was compensated by the king for the loss of tythes paid by those who had lived on the 50 acres of parish land which was enclosed by a fence and ditch to make the park. John Trop was paid 3d a day as custodian of the park and for maintenance of the beasts kept there – deer, most likely.

Sadly, the magnificent Le Herber did not last long. As mentioned above, Gravesend had become a vital port and the king's fine manor also attracted a lot of notice. England was still at war with France and her allies, the Castilians. In August 1380, a Castilian fleet sailed up the Thames, set Gravesend alight – including the king's manor – and took many Gravesendians captive. The town burned, although St Mary's church, well away from the riverside, survived undamaged. The people were left destitute and blamed the king for having built his manor as such an obvious target with no means of defending it. (There were no forts or blockhouses then.) It was hardly the fault of young King Richard II – grandson of Edward III – where the previous king had chosen to build, but relations with the new king grew worse.

A year after the fire came the Peasants' Revolt in June 1381. King

Richard, aged 14, arrived at Gravesend by boat from London. Why he came, we don't know but it's recorded that 'not liking the shabby appearance of the inhabitants', he was afraid to land and was rowed back upriver to the Tower of London. Perhaps the people were shabby because they'd lost everything in the fire or, more likely, the king thought they might be supporters of Wat Tyler.

However, Gravesend made an appeal to King Richard, asking aid for the town, so it could rebuild. Perhaps remembering how 'shabby' the place was, Richard granted the watermen of Gravesend the sole right to ferry passengers to London: extending the traditional rights of Gravesend watermen to operate what was known as the "Long Ferry". This right was confirmed by later monarchs and gave great impetus to the growth of Gravesend as a maritime centre and port. But what Richard gave with one hand he took away with the other. A year later (1383), he granted all the rents from the manor lands in Gravesend, having demolished the gutted manor itself, and the lands of neighbouring Parrock Manor in Milton Parish to the Abbot of St Mary Graces in London. So the rents now went to pay for the upkeep of an abbey, instead of more local beneficiaries. On top of that, customs duties were now levied at a ha'penny a cauldron on coal landed at Gravesend. The money raised by making it more expensive to off-load coal here, rather than anywhere else, also went straight to London to pay for repairs to London Bridge.

In 1399, when Richard II was ousted from his throne by his cousin Henry IV, he was brought by river as a prisoner to Gravesend, under guard, and briefly imprisoned here while Henry decided what to do with him. I don't suppose Richard got much sympathy from the Gravesendians before he was taken on to Leeds Castle for a while. He finished up in Pontefract Castle and died there, soon after, in mysterious circumstances. Fortunately for Gravesend, in 1401, Henry IV confirmed the villagers' right of the Long Ferry.

6

∾

The High Street and The Market

The High Street still marks the boundary between the parishes of Milton and Gravesend which means the later Town Hall and Law Courts on the eastern side have always been in Milton, not Gravesend at all. The earliest known mention of the High Street is in 1334 when property was conveyed to John Page, the younger, and Helen, his wife, of Gravesend. This was in the parish of Milton and stated as 'abutting upon High Street towards the west'. According to a document of 1456, between the old Town Hall and the river there were only two houses on the Milton side of the street with one or two tenements on the Town Quay. It is probable that a channel ran down the middle of the street and where unwanted domestic rubbish and effluent was emptied to run down to the river. The town's Second Charter dated 1568, required every inhabitant 'to weekly cleanse before his door for the avoidance of evil odours under a penalty of 3s 4d'.

Between the Kent Public House and the junction with Royal Pier Road was land belonging to the Abbot of the Monastery of St. Mary Le Graces,

Tower Hill, London. This was also part of the old manor of Parrock (see below). The land between the Kent Pub and Bank Street was, in the early part of the 15th century, the site of Dame Anne's Hall. On the other side of Bank Street there was a property known as 'Beelings' (or Baldwin's Acre) and the rest of the land to the north was called Stonehawe or Stonehall.

The market had originally been established in 1268 by a grant given by Henry III to his faithful servant Robert de la Parrock of Parrock Manor. In 1366, a second charter granted by Edward III established a market for the 'Men of the Town' independently from the manor and the day was changed to Thursday. It was this charter that gave the town its coat of arms – a boat with a mast rowed by hooded rowers and steered by a porcupine.

By 1562, it was suggested that the adjoining parishes of Milton and Gravesend were in decline because they did not have a market for both parishes. The response was a new Charter of Incorporation for the two parishes in 1568 which changed the day of the market to Wednesday and stipulated that a three day fair was to be held in January.

Standing at the river edge at the foot of the High Street is one of the oldest taverns in the country, now called The Three Daws. This ancient inn was converted from five traditional timber fronted cottages. It can be dated back to the 15th century when it was known as 'The Three Choughs', which was the badge of St Thomas Becket, and after the Reformation as 'The Cornish Choughs' - although it didn't gain its licence until the 1560s.

7

∽

The People of Milton Parish

There is a document, called a rental, for the manor of Meltone by Gravesend (Milton), drawn up in January 1393. It makes fascinating reading because it gives the names of all the tenants of the manor and how much land they rented. It begins by saying that the Lord of Parrock Manor – actually the Abbot of St Mary Graces in London – must pay the king 58s a year in four equal instalments – at Easter, St John's day (midsummer), Michaelmas (in September) and Christmas. In addition, at Christmas, the lord was to send 2 lbs pepper (an exotic and expensive import) and 14 chickens for the royal Christmas dinner.

The most important tenants in Milton were John Page, John Gravesend and William Rodyon. Page was the king's Searcher of the Thames – a customs officer – and he owned 12 acres and a messuage. A messuage was a plot of land big enough to build a house on and you paid the rent whether you built the house or not. John Gravesend owned over 10 acres and his surname suggests he was an important man in town (although I haven't discovered why) and William Rodyon had 9 acres. Other tenants had a messuage and no extra land: people like William Wade, John Abell and Sabina Stace – the only woman named as a Milton tenant.

Quite a few tenants are listed, not by name but as someone's heirs, so the heir of Adam atte Noke, the heir of John atte Wode and the heirs of William Colle all rented just 3 rods of land each. This suggests that the turnover among the poorer tenants was such that it was difficult to keep track of the heirs. Plague might have been the cause. Names that crop up more than once suggest families or relatives: the Pages, atte Barres, Colles, Ballingers, Jervays, Abells and atte Nokes. In all, the list accounts for 49 tenants which, along with wives and children and folk who weren't tenants, probably took the population of Milton close to the magic number of 300 that would have made it a town. Gravesend probably came even closer to qualifying as Milton is referred to as 'by Gravesend', suggesting that in 1393, Gravesend was the bigger of the two.

8

~

Parrock Manor, Milton

Parrock Manor took its name from Robert de Parrock (or Paddock) who owned it in 1268. Descended from Stephen de Gravesend, a knight of King Edward I, the Bishop of London, also named Stephen de Gravesend, came to own it. When he died in 1338, his kinsman, Sir Thomas de Gravesend, inherited it. Sir Thomas, born in 1314, was probably the bishop's nephew, the son of his brother, Richard de Gravesend. Thomas and his wife, Joan, were living at the manor in 1375 when tragedy struck because it seems the whole family, including their only daughter, Cecily, and granddaughter, Joan, all died upon the feast of St Margaret of Antioch on the 20th July. Maybe they caught the plague. As a result, Parrock Manor passed to the Crown.

Nothing much remains of the manor today except for a few stones of the gatehouse in Joy Road and the name 'Old Manor Drive' behind Echo Square but more significant is 'The Warren' beside Valley Drive, once part of the manor parklands where Sir Thomas's rabbits roamed.

Three Bishops. Gravesend was the birthplace of three bishops who were proud of it and used it as their surname. Richard de Gravesend, Treasurer of Hereford Diocese, Archdeacon of Oxford and Dean of Lincoln Cathedral was elected as Bishop of Lincoln in September 1258 and consecrated at Canterbury in November. Unfortunately for Richard, he supported Simon de Montfort in the Barons' War of 1263-65 and when de Montfort was slain at the battle of Evesham and the cause lost in 1265, the bishop was suspended from office and sent into exile by King Henry III. However, he was pardoned and back in Lincoln two years later, continuing in office until his death in December 1279.

The Bishop of Lincoln had a nephew, also called Richard de Gravesend, who followed his uncle into the Church but his history is uncertain. He was probably Prebend of Totenhall in the diocese of London, Archdeacon of Essex and, possibly, of Northampton as well. What is certain is that the younger Richard was elected as Bishop of London in May 1280 and enthroned in St Paul's Cathedral in October that year. He served as bishop until his death in December 1303.

But the story doesn't end there because in 1318, Stephen de Gravesend follows *his* uncle as Bishop of Lincoln. Along with other churchmen: William Melton, Archbishop of York; Hamo de Hythe, Bishop of Rochester, and John Ross, Bishop of Carlisle, Stephen was one of the few who spoke in favour of Edward II in 1326 when Parliament deposed the king. It was Stephen who owned Nurstead Manor and Parrock Manor until his death in 1338.

9

～

Randall Manor, Shorne

When the ancient Saxon village of Merston (Lower Shorne) was falling into decay, a new manor grew within the parish boundaries. From early times the de Cobham family had held lands in Shorne. In 1287, John de Cobham died and his two sons divided the estates between them. The manor of Randall in Shorne was Henry de Cobham's share and this is the first time the manor is named. In the early 14th century it seems a 3s 4d share of the manor belonged to the Abbess of Fontevrand, Edmund de Pakenham's share was worth 7 shillings a year and the remainder, some 120 acres of arable land, 20 acres of pasture, 5 acres of wood, 80 acres of salt marsh and a windmill, first introduced in around 1200, was held by Roger de Northwood to the value of 35 shillings a year. When Henry de Cobham acquired the manor of Randall, he made it his home and for a couple of generations members of the de Cobham family rode out from Randall as sheriffs, knights of the shire, lords of parliament, or to join the king's army.

The manor house has disappeared but the site is still identifiable. Today, under a tangle of roots and coppiced woodland, traces of the old building show it had substantial stone foundations standing on a rectangular plateau surrounded on three sides by a moat and fishponds. Lying in a valley on the north side of Randall Heath, it was protected to the south and west by the high ground of the heath and looked out to the north over the fishpond (about half an acre) to a distant view of the Thames.

Archaeological excavations on the site show that it was probably on the site of an earlier building, the rebuilding being late 13th or early 14th century. The remains of a large medieval stone hearth, surrounded by tiles set on edge, was also found. In the kitchen, archaeologists found a beehive-shaped construction made of chalk. Although it looked rather like an oven there was no sign that it had ever been heated. One archaeologist put his can of fizzy drink inside it during a sudden July shower and later found his drink had been beautifully chilled as the rain evaporated from the wet chalk – it was a medieval fridge!

Henry de Cobham married a rich heiress, Joan, the daughter of Stephen de Penchester, through whom he acquired Allington Castle and other estates. He was elected as knight of the shire (an MP) in 1307. He earned royal favour because of his personal bravery in the wars of King Edward I against the Welsh and Scots. He was made a knight banneret in the field for gallantry at the siege of Calaverock in Scotland in 1300 (a banneret is a promotion from a knight bachelor). Following this, Henry was sheriff of Kent on many occasions. When Edward I died, Henry supported Edward II against the barons and because of his loyalty he was created Lord of Randall and received a writ of summons to the Lords in the year before his death. He also built Randall Chapel (now the south chancel) at Shorne church and his effigy still rests in the rebuilt chapel. The helmet on which the effigy's head rests is interesting because its interior is carefully carved to show the method of fitting and padding the helmet, not unlike the padding of a modern crash helmet.

On Henry's death, his son, Sir Stephen, succeeded to the barony and for a hundred years the manor was an important part of the life of Shorne village, although after a few generations it was usually occupied by nephews and nieces of the main line of the family. In 1368, Thomas Morice, a wealthy lawyer, left to his son-in-law, Sir Thomas de Cobham, his leasehold on Randall manor and his armour.

10

~

St. George's Church, Gravesend

When King Edward III built his riverside manor of Le Herber in Gravesend in the 1360s, he included a separate private chapel so he didn't have to traipse all the way to St Mary's to pray alongside the common folk. He dedicated the new chapel to his favourite saint: George, who was becoming accepted as England's patron saint around that time.

In 1434 a severe winter frost on the Thames, starting on Christmas Day and lasting until 5th February 1435, caused great hardship to the watermen of Gravesend. In 1475, with the king's manor itself no longer standing and Gravesend centring its business more and more on the riverside, the villagers petitioned the king, Edward IV, to let them use his chapel of St George for regular services. The king agreed but it was stipulated by the Bishop of Rochester that for christenings and funerals they would still have to use St Mary's near the old Dover Road.

As mentioned above, in 1508, St Mary's had a serious fire and St George's chapel was used while the old parish church was being repaired. However, it seems that Gravesendians preferred St George's, being more convenient, and the rebuilding of St Mary's was done so badly that although the bishop reconsecrated it in April 1510 – the day after he consecrated St George's as a fully fledged church, St Mary's was in ruins again just twenty years later. This time, nobody seems to have bothered to repair it and in 1544 St George's became the official parish church. By now it would have been a Protestant church. Since the last burial in St Mary's churchyard took place as late as 1598, in the reign of Elizabeth I, it seems as though one or two folk still clung quietly to the now-illegal Roman Catholic religion. Between 1532 and 1545, money was raised to build a steeple on St George's, though the church burned down in August 1727 when 110 houses in the High Street were engulfed in flames. So nothing remains of medieval St George's church either.

11

⌢

Wombwell Hall, Northfleet

Durndale Manor in Hall Road was bought in 1461 by Thomas Wombwell of Wombwell in Yorkshire from the Wainford family of South-fleet. He had fought alongside Edward IV at the battle of Towton on 29th March that year and may have been rewarded after the victory with money to buy the manor. Ten years later, he had built the first Wombwell Hall. The Wombwell family website says he was married to Catherine Inglesby but, in his will, written on 4th September 1483, Thomas left 'all my goods not bequeathed elsewhere to William Swan of Gravesend, Joan my wife and John my son' – these three were also named as his executors. Joan was to have Durndale and everything that went with it. Now calling himself Thomas Wombwell of Northfleet, he wanted to be buried in St Botolph's church, leaving 6s 8d for church repairs. He left 4 quarters of barley each to Thomas Raynold, Thomas Hills, John Hills and to his kinswomen Alice Pegot and Alice Wombwell. He bequeathed 2 cows to his kinsman John Wombwell and a bullock to Alice Clerk. His household servants got a shilling each, his daughters Margaret and Alice both received £20 and another daughter Elizabeth was to have 20 marks.

Also in Thomas's will, we discover that he owned land in Ash, Meopham, Denton and Chalk, all of which went to his wife until her death, then to his son John, except for 4 acres that were left to John Arncliff – who witnessed the will along with John Horspullen, vicar of Northfleet, and Hugh Wombwell, a chaplain who may have been Thomas's son. Other land at Ash went to another son, William. Thomas Wombwell died before May 1484, when his will went to probate.

12

～～

The Battle of Gravesend, 1483

As Richard III reached Lincoln in September 1483, news came that the southern counties of England were rising in revolt and the leader of the uprising was, unaccountably, the king's most trusted supporter, the Duke of Buckingham. No satisfactory explanation for Buckingham's astounding change of allegiance has ever come to light. Having insisted with such enthusiasm that Richard take the crown only a few months earlier and been rewarded with the utmost generosity by a king who could hardly afford it, his change of heart was a mystery bordering on madness. Richard could hardly believe what he was told and called Buckingham 'the most untrue creature living', which was a serious rebuke in those days.

The rebellion was intended to be a co-ordinated uprising on two fronts: one in Kent where Buckingham held various estates, including Tonbridge, Penshurst and Sutton Valence; the other on the Welsh borders and in the South-West which were the duke's key strongholds. The rising was said to be in support of the late King Edward's bastard sons, known as The

Princes in the Tower who were living at the Tower to which Buckingham, as Constable of England, had free access.

But the rebellion went wrong from the start. The Kentish uprising happened a week too early, on 10th October, before the Welsh and South-Western end of things was ready. This allowed the two parts to be dealt with one at a time, making it easy for a clever military strategist like King Richard to put down the revolt. The Duke of Norfolk sent John Brooke, Lord Cobham; John Middleton and John Norbury with a contingent of 100 men to hold Gravesend and the passage across the Thames to Essex against the rebels.

On October 13th, there was a riot in Gravesend as John Bonting, another official sent by Norfolk to quash the uprising, joined the rebels instead, killing a number of men who were supposedly his fellows. The revolt was eventually put down but King Richard worried about the loyalty of Kent because Sandwich, Rochester, Maidstone, Tonbridge and now Gravesend and Dartford had all been centres of insurrection that autumn. In Sandwich, Robert Brent, appointed by the Crown as the port's Controller of Customs and in Canterbury a previous sheriff, Alderman George Brown, were both indicted for treason although George Brown died before his trial.

After subduing the rising in Kent, the king then hurried to the South-West personally to face Buckingham and what was expected to be a bigger and more dangerous uprising, now claimed to be in aid of putting Henry Tudor (later henry VII) on the throne. But the weather – or God – was on this occasion in Richard's favour. Storms and the subsequent flooding washed away bridges, making rivers impassable so the Welsh and South-Western contingents could not combine and the rebellion was washed away. Buckingham was captured, tried for treason and executed, taking to the grave the reasons behind his treachery.

Timeline

1066 (William I) – 1485 (Henry VII)

1066 – William I invades England at Battle of Hastings

1086 – Gravesend appears in the Domesday Book as 'Gravesham'. The manor belonged to Odo, Bishop of Bayeux

1125 – In Textus Roffensis, GRAVESÆNDE; from the Saxon word Gerefa, a ruler, or portreve.

1151 – Benedictine nunnery founded at Higham. The first prioress to be appointed was Mary de Bois, daughter of King Stephen

1168 – Lime carried from Gravesend to Dover for work on Dover Castle.

1180 – Normans built large squat tower for St. Botolph's Church, Northfleet

1201 – Archbishop Hubert gave King John 4 palfreys (a small saddle horse for ladies) in return for the privilege of holding a ten-day fair at Northfleet

1208 – The seat of the de Cobham family established at Cobham

1210 – Reverend Adam first recorded Rector of Gravesend.

1219 – Manor of Gravesend worth £15 held by Richard de Halstede. Manor of Parrock worth 5 marks

1240 – John Baker and James Marecall of Gravesend avoided duty when selling wine

1248 – Sir Henry de Cramaville holds Gravesend Manor

1258 – Richard de Gravesend, Bishop of Lincoln

1268 – Robert de la Parock leased Parrock Manor from William de Clovil.

1268 – A charter for a market was conferred on Robert de la Parrock

1268 – Town status was granted to Gravesend and Milton.

1268 – The first Mayor of Gravesend was elected.

1282 – Richard de Gravesend becomes Bishop of Lincoln

1293 – Gravesend watermen first given the right to operate the "Long Ferry" to London

1318 – Stephen de Gravesend becomes Bishop of London

1377 – A beacon erected on what is now Windmill Hill was instituted by King Richard II.

1377 – French and Spanish forces attack and burn Gravesend and capture many inhabitants

1380 – Grant of exclusive rights to Gravesend watermen for a 'Long Ferry' extended by Richard II

1435 – Severe winter frost on the Thames from 25th December 1434 until 5th February, caused great hardship to the watermen of Gravesend

1445 – Date of the "Christopher Inn" near the Town Quay, on the site of the present Pier Hotel

1450 – Northfleet men pardoned after Jack Cade's rebellion - they "fought lustily"

1451 – First mention of bridge across the River Fleet at Northfleet

1456 – High Street, Gravesend was known as "King's Way"

1461 – Grant of the Long Ferry renewed by Edward IV

1461 – Thomas Wombwell bought an estate at Northfleet

1471 – Wombwell Hall built by Thomas Wombwell.

1483 – "Battle of Gravesend" as part of the Buckingham rebellion against Richard III

1485 – Henry VII defeats Richard III at the Battle of Bosworth

Basic timeline courtesy of www.discovergravesham.co.uk/gravesend-chronology/gravesend-chronology.html

Acknowledgements

I'm grateful for all the information shared by local parishes and organisations about their history. A great source for further local research would be the Discover Gravesham website and the local studies department at Gravesend Central Library, Windmill Street, Gravesend.

Toni Mount
MA, BA (Hons)
Dip European Humanities,
Dip Lit & Creative Writing, Cert Ed

I'm a history teacher, a writer, and an enthusiastic life-long-learner. I'm a member of the Richard III Society's Research Committee and two local Creative Writing groups.

I attended Gravesend Grammar School and originally worked as a scientist at Burroughs Wellcome in Dartford.

I earned my Masters degree from the University of Kent in 2009, studying a medieval medical manuscript at the Wellcome Library in London. My BA (with First-class Honours), my Diploma in Literature and Creative Writing and my Diploma in European Humanities are from the Open University. My Certificate in Education (Post-Compulsory Education and Training) is from the University of Greenwich.

I teach history at my own weekly classes via ZOOM and online at Medieval-Courses.com

Books by Toni Mount

My first book for Amberley Publishing, *Everyday Life in Medieval London*, was published in 2014 and became an Amazon best seller. I also wrote *The Medieval Housewife and other Women of the 15th Century* and *Dragon's Blood & Willow Bark - the mysteries of medieval medicine* for Amberley That book was subsequently republished in paperback and renamed *Medieval Medicine its Mysteries and Science*. Also, in 2016 *A Year in the life of Medieval England* was published and I have written a biography of Isaac Newton for Amberley Books.

More recently I've written *How to Survive in Medieval England* for Pen & Sword Books which has become an Amazon Best Seller and also *How to Survive in Tudor England* and *How to Survive in Anglo-Saxon England*, with more to come.

In 2016 my first novel, a medieval murder mystery *The Colour of Poison* was published by MadeGlobal Publishing and introduced my would-be sleuth, Sebastian Foxley. This has now become as successful 12 book series with over 40,000 copies sold.

Milton Keynes UK
Ingram Content Group UK Ltd.
UKHW050856070424
440639UK00006BA/33